ELIJAH
Leader Guide

A Bible Study by

Melissa Spoelstra

Elijah

Spiritual Stamina
in Every Season

LEADER GUIDE
Jenny Youngman, Contributor

Abingdon Women / Nashville

ELIJAH
Spiritual Stamina in Every Season
Leader Guide

ISBN 978-1-5018-3893-4

18 19 20 21 22 23 24 25 26 27—10 9 8 7 6 5 4 3 2 1
MANUFACTURED IN THE UNITED STATES OF AMERICA

Contents

About the Author 6

Introduction 7

Getting Started 11

Tips for Tackling Five Common Challenges 15

Basic Leader Helps 21

Introductory Session 23

Week 1: Prayer
      1 Kings 17 26

Week 2: Choices
      1 Kings 18:1-40 31

Week 3: Soul Care
      1 Kings 18:41–19:18 36

Week 4: Surrender
      1 Kings 19:19–22:9 41

Week 5: Mentoring
      2 Kings 1–2 46

Week 6: Legacy
      Elijah in the Old and New Testaments 51

Bonus: Thirty Days of Prayer Challenge 56

Video Viewer Guide Answers 61

Notes 62

About the Author

Melissa Spoelstra is a popular women's conference speaker (including the Aspire Women's Events), Bible teacher, and writer who is madly in love with Jesus and passionate about studying God's Word and helping women of all ages seek Christ and know Him more intimately through serious Bible study. Having a degree in Bible theology, she enjoys teaching God's Word to the body of Christ and traveling to diverse groups and churches across the nation, even to Nairobi, Kenya, for a women's prayer conference. Melissa is the author of the Bible studies *Numbers: Learning Contentment in a Culture of More*; *First Corinthians: Living Love When We Disagree*; *Joseph: The Journey to Forgiveness*; *Jeremiah: Daring to Hope in an Unstable World*; and the parenting books *Total Family Makeover: 8 Steps to Making Disciples at Home* and *Total Christmas Makeover: 31 Devotions to Celebrate with Purpose*. She has published articles in *ParentLife*, *Women's Spectrum*, and *Just Between Us*, and writes a regular blog in which she shares her musings about what God is teaching her on any given day. She lives in Dublin, Ohio, with her pastor husband, Sean, and their four kids: Zach, Abby, Sara, and Rachel.

Follow Melissa:

 @MelSpoelstra

 @Daring2Hope

 @AuthorMelissaSpoelstra

Her blog   MelissaSpoelstra.com
            (check here also for event dates and booking information)

Introduction

We connect with Elijah on so many levels. Like him, we have seen God show up in real ways. God has encouraged us, comforted us, provided for us, and shown Himself real to us through His Word, His presence, and His activity in our lives. Other times the brook has seemed to dry up, and we've been unable to make sense of another challenge, disappointment, or frustration. Sometimes these ups and downs are less momentary and more like seasons. Through all the highs and lows—and especially those times when we want to quit—we need to stay true to our faith and calling if we want to live fully and finish well. We need spiritual stamina not only to endure but also to thrive as we carry out the unique mission God has for each of us.

In this study, your group will examine the ministry of Elijah, who came to be considered "the great prophet, the man who stands as the pattern for other prophets." [1] Over the next six weeks we'll learn some of the spiritual stamina secrets that helped him hold on and persevere in faith, including practical habits related to the following areas:

1. prayer
2. choices
3. soul care
4. surrender
5. mentoring
6. legacy

Together we'll see that finishing well was Elijah's greatest legacy, and we'll explore how to make that our legacy too. Starting is easy, but finishing well requires stamina!

About the Participant Book

Before the first session, you will want to distribute copies of the participant book to the members of your group. Be sure to communicate that they are to complete the first week of readings *before* your first group session. For each week there are five readings or lessons that combine study of Scripture with personal reflection and application (**orange type** indicates write-in-the-book questions and activities). Each lesson ends with a "Talk with God" prayer suggestion.

On average you will need about twenty to thirty minutes to complete each lesson. Completing these readings each week will prepare the women for the discussion and activities of the group session.

About This Leader Guide

As you gather each week with the members of your group, you will have the opportunity to watch a video, discuss and respond to what you're learning, and pray together. You will need access to a television and DVD player with working remotes.

Creating a warm and inviting atmosphere will help to make the women feel welcome. Although optional, you might consider providing snacks for your first meeting and inviting group members to rotate in bringing refreshments each week.

This leader guide and the DVD will be your primary tools for leading your group on this journey to learn how to have spiritual stamina. Whether you choose to follow this guide step by step, modify its contents to meet your group's needs and preferences, or simply peruse it to find a few helpful tips, questions, and ideas, you will find in these pages some valuable tools for creating a successful group experience.

Getting Started: This is a list of strategies, options, and introductory information that will help you ensure good organization and communication. You will want to review this material and communicate relevant information to group members prior to your group session for Week 1, either via e-mail or in an introductory session (see more about this in Getting Started). Or you might consider adding fifteen to thirty minutes to your first session for reviewing some of these important housekeeping details. Whichever option you choose, be sure that group members have the opportunity to purchase books and complete Week 1 before your session for Week 1.

Tips for Tackling Five Common Challenges: This section includes ideas for addressing recurring issues that come up when leading a group. Every leader knows that some group dynamics can be difficult to tackle. What will you do when one person dominates the discussion or cuts off another person who is speaking? All eyes will be on you to see how you will intervene or ignore these situations. Be sure to check out these five common challenges and ideas to help when you encounter them.

Basic Leader Helps: This list of basic leader tips will help you to prepare for and lead each group session.

Session Outlines: Six adaptable outlines are provided to help guide your group time each week. Each begins with a "Leader Prep" section to assist with preparation.

Preview: Thirty-Day Prayer Challenge: At the end of this book, you'll find information about the bonus thirty-day prayer challenge. If you and/or your group choose to participate in this challenge, you will commit to spend ten extra minutes in prayer each day using one of two resources: (1) free downloadable introductions to different prayer methods or approaches, which you may use throughout the thirty days (also included on pages 56-60 for your review), or (2) the book 30 *Days of Prayer for Spiritual Stamina* (members of your group may download the free resources or order the book by going to www.abingdonwomen.com/Elijah).

This study is designed for six weeks, with an optional introductory session. Or, if desired, you may choose to extend the study to eight or twelve weeks; see the options included in Getting Started. Again, whichever option you choose, be sure that group members have the opportunity to purchase participant books and complete Week 1 before your session for Week 1.

Each of the session outlines in this book may be used for a 60-minute, 90-minute, or 120-minute session. The following formats are offered as templates that you may modify for your group:

60-Minute Format
Welcome/Fellowship (2 minutes)
All Play (3–5 minutes)
Prayer (2 minutes)
Video (25–30 minutes)
Group Discussion (20 minutes)
Prayer Requests (3 minutes)

90-Minute Format
Welcome/Fellowship (5–10 minutes)
All Play (3–5 minutes)
Prayer (2 minutes)
Video (25–30 minutes)
Group Discussion (25 minutes)
Optional Group Activity (5–10 minutes)
Prayer Requests (5–8 minutes)

120-Minute Format

Welcome/Fellowship (10–12 minutes)
All Play (5–10 minutes)
Prayer (3 minutes)
Video (25–30 minutes)
Group Discussion (30–35 minutes)
Optional Group Activity (10 minutes)
Prayer Requests (15–20 minutes)

As you can see, the basic elements remain the same in each format: a welcome/fellowship time, an "All Play" icebreaker question that everyone can answer, a video segment, group discussion, and prayer time. The 90-minute and 120-minute options offer longer times for fellowship, discussion, and prayer plus an optional group activity. If you choose not to do the group activity, you may add that time to another element of the session, such as group discussion or prayer. (See Getting Started for notes about including food, planning for childcare, and other important organizational details.)

If you are new to leading Bible studies and/or would like to have a framework to follow, the session outlines will guide you. Note that more discussion questions have been provided than you may have time to include. Before the session, choose the questions you want to cover and put a check mark beside them. Page references are provided for those questions that relate to questions or activities in the participant book. For these questions, invite group members to turn in their participant books to the pages indicated.

If you are a seasoned group leader looking only for a few good questions or ideas, I encourage you to take what you want and leave the rest. After all, you know your group better than I do! Ask God to show you what areas to focus on from the week's homework and use my discussion outline as a template that you can revise.

Of course, the Holy Spirit knows the content of this study (His Word) and the women in your group better than anyone, so above all I encourage you to lead this study under the Holy Spirit's direction, allowing yourself the freedom to make any changes or adaptations that are helpful or desirable.

I'm so excited that God has called you to lead a group of ladies through a study of the prophet Elijah's life. Know that I am praying for you and believing God for the work He will do through your leadership. Now, let's get started!

Getting Started

Before your study begins, be sure to review the following introductory information that will help you ensure good organization and communication. You are encouraged to communicate relevant information such as the dates, times, and location for group meetings; when/where/how to purchase books; details regarding childcare and food; expectations and ground rules; and an overview of the study to group members during an introductory session or via e-mail before your session for Week 1.

1. Determine the length of your study. The basic study is designed for six weeks (plus an optional introductory session), but you also can plan for an eight- or twelve-week study.
   - For a six-week study—plus an additional (optional) introductory session if desired—use the session guides in this book and the video segments on the DVD. Be sure to distribute books during the introductory session if you are having one or prior to your session for Week 1.
   - For an eight-week study, add both an introductory session and a closing celebration. In the introductory session, watch the introductory video message and spend time getting to know one another, presenting basic housekeeping information, and praying together (use the guide on pages 23–25). For a closing celebration, discuss what you have learned together in a special gathering that includes refreshments or perhaps a brunch, luncheon, or supper. A closing celebration provides an excellent opportunity for ongoing groups to invite friends and reach out to others who might be interested in joining the group for a future study.
   - To allow more time for completing homework, extend the study to twelve weeks. This is especially helpful for groups with mothers of young children or women carrying a heavy work or ministry schedule. With this option, women have two weeks in which to complete each week of homework in the participant book. In your group sessions, watch and discuss the video the

first week; then review and discuss homework the next week. Some women find they are better able to complete assignments and digest what they are learning this way.

2. Determine the length of each group session (60, 90, or 120 minutes). See the format templates outlined on pages 9–10.

3. Decide ahead of time if you/your church will purchase participant books that group members can buy in advance during an introductory session or in advance of your first session, or if group members will buy their own books individually. If you expect each member to buy her own book, e-mail group members purchasing information (be sure to note the cost, including tax and shipping if applicable). Consider including online links as well. Be sure to allow enough time for participants to purchase books and complete the readings for Week 1 prior to your session for Week 1.

4. Create a group roster that includes each group member's name, e-mail, mailing address, and primary phone number. (Collect this information through registration, e-mail, or an introductory session.) Distribute copies of the roster to group members prior to or during your first session. A group roster enables group members to stay connected and contact one another freely as needed, such as when taking a meal or sending a card to someone who is sick, who has missed several group sessions, or who has had a baby or another significant life event. Group members may want to meet for coffee or lunch to follow up on things shared in the study as well. As women cry and laugh and share life together in a Bible study, their lives will be intertwined, even if only for a short time.

5. Make decisions about childcare and food and communicate this information to group members in advance. Will childcare be offered, and will there be a cost associated with it? Will refreshments be served at your gatherings? (Note: If your group is meeting for sixty minutes, you will not have time for a formal fellowship time with refreshments. You might consider having refreshments set up early and inviting women to come a few minutes before the session officially begins.) If you choose to have food, the introductory meeting is a good time to pass around a sign-up sheet. In the Bible study group I lead, we like to eat, so we have three women sign up to bring food for each meeting. One brings fruit, another brings bread or muffins, and another brings an egg dish. Your group may want to keep it simple; just be mindful of food allergies and provide choices.

6. Let group members know what to expect. Those who have never participated in a women's Bible study group may be intimidated, scared, or unsure of what to expect. Friends have told me that when they first came to Bible study, they were concerned they would be called on to pray out loud or expected to know everything in the Bible. Ease group members' concerns up front. Reassure the women that they will not be put on the spot and that they may choose to share as they are comfortable. Encourage participation while fostering a "safe" environment. Laying a few basic ground rules such as these can help you to achieve this kind of environment:

    *   *Confidentiality.* Communicate that anything shared in the group is not to be repeated outside of those present in the study. Women need to feel safe to be vulnerable and authentic.
    *   *Sensitivity.* Talk about courtesy, which includes practices such as refraining from interrupting, monopolizing, or trying to "fix" shared problems. Women want to be heard, not told what to do, when they share an issue in their lives. If they have advice to share with an individual, ask them to speak with the person privately after study. When studying God's Word, some differences of opinion are bound to arise as to interpretation and/or application. This is a good place to sharpen one another and respectfully disagree so that you may grow and understand different viewpoints. Remind the women that it's okay to question and see things differently; however, they must be kind and sensitive to the feelings of others.
    *   *Purpose.* The primary reason you are taking time out of your busy schedules to meet together is to study the Bible. Though your group will pray for, serve, and support one another, your primary focus is to study the Bible. You learn in community from one another as you draw near to God through His Word. Though you may want to plan a service or social activity during the course of your study, these times should be secondary to your study time together. If group members express a desire for the group to do more outreach, service, or socials, gently remind them of the primary reason you gather.

7. Before the study begins, provide a short preview of the study's content, summarizing highlights in an e-mail or introductory session. You might whet the appetite for what is to come by sharing (or reading) parts of the introduction from the participant book. Consider sharing a personal story that relates to the study's theme. What has been happening in your life recently that has given you an opportunity to develop spiritual stamina? As you are enthusiastic about getting into God's Word together, your members will catch your contagious desire to grow in stamina in every season.

8. If you are having an introductory session, show the introductory video and open the floor for women to share in response to the questions on pages 24–25.

9. Be sure to communicate to participants that they are to read Week 1 in the participant book prior to your session for Week 1. Review the options for study found in the introduction to the participant book and encourage participants to choose the options they plan to complete and then share this information with someone in the group for accountability.

Tips for Tackling Five Common Challenges

Challenge #1: Preparation

Do you know that feeling when Bible study is in two days and you haven't even finished the homework, much less prepared for the group session? We've all been there. When I'm unprepared, I can sense the difference when I'm teaching Sunday school, leading VBS, or facilitating discussion in my women's Bible study group. I'm hurried, scattered, and less confident when I haven't dedicated the proper time for preparation. It doesn't take hours, but it does take commitment.

I check myself with a little acronym when I prepare to lead: S-S-S. Many years ago I was asked to lead a segment on teacher training for a group of VBS leaders. I remember asking the Lord, "What are the most important things to remember when we handle your Word to teach?" As I sat listening, He gave me this process of S-S-S that has stuck with me through the years. It looks like this:

S—Savior. Know your Savior. We must spend time talking, listening, and staying closely connected with Jesus in order to lead well. As we intentionally keep our walk with Him close and vibrant, we can then hear His voice about how to structure our lesson, what questions to ask, and which verses in His Word to focus on.

S—Story. Know your story. Though God has been gracious to me when I have winged it, I feel the most freedom with God's truth when I have prepared thoroughly. Try not to cram in multiple days of homework at one time. Let it sink into your soul by reading curiously and slowly. Go back to areas that especially strike you and allow God to use His Word in your heart and mind so that you can teach with authenticity. Women can tell when you are flying by the seat of your pants.

S—Students. Know your students. Who are these women God has given you to shepherd? Are they struggling with finances, relationships, or body-image issues? Are they mature Christ-followers who need to be challenged to go deeper in their study of God's Word or seekers who need extra explanations about where the books of the Bible are located? Most likely, you will be teaching to a wide range of backgrounds as well as emotional and spiritual maturity levels, and you will need God's wisdom and guidance to inspire them.

Challenge #2: Group Dynamics

Have you experienced that uncomfortable feeling when you ask a discussion question and a long silence settles over the group? With your eyes begging someone to break the ice, you wonder if you should let the question linger or jump in with your own answer. Other problems with group dynamics surface when Silent Suzy never contributes to the conversation because Talking Tammy answers every question. What does a good leader do in these situations? While every group has a unique vibe, I have found these general concepts very helpful in facilitating discussion:

First of all, a good leader asks questions. Jesus was our greatest example. He definitely taught spiritual truths, but one of His most effective methods was asking questions. Proverbs 20:5 says, "Though good advice lies deep within the heart, / a person with understanding will draw it out." As leaders, we must be intentional askers and listeners. I try to gauge myself throughout the discussion by reflecting often on this simple question: "Am I doing all the talking?" When I find I am hearing my own voice too much, I make a point to ask and listen more. Even if waiting means a little silence hangs in the air, eventually someone will pipe up and share. Women learn from one another's insights and experiences; we rob them of others' comments when we monopolize as leaders.

Now what about Talking Tammy? She not only answers every question but also makes a comment after each woman shares something (often relating to one of her own experiences). Try one of these transitional statements:

- "Thanks Tammy, let's see if someone else has some insight as well."
- "Let's hear from someone who hasn't shared yet today."
- "Is there anyone who hasn't talked much today who would be willing to answer this question?"

The hope is that Talking Tammy will realize that she has had a lot of floor time.

Sometimes Talking Tammy also struggles to "land the plane." She can't find a stopping place in her story. Help her out by jumping in when she takes a breath and make a summary statement for her. For example, "I hear you saying that you could relate to Elijah's weariness. Does anyone else find Elijah's experience resonating in a similar way?"

Occasionally I have had to take someone aside in a loving way and address her amount of talking. Pray hard and be gentle, but address the issue. As a leader, you must keep in mind the good of the group as a whole.

I once had several ladies leave the group because they were so frustrated by the continual barrage of talking by one woman in particular. Some of her many comments were insensitive and offensive to others in the room. I don't like confrontation, so I didn't want to address it. However, God grew me as a leader to speak loving truth even when it hurts for the benefit of those we are called to shepherd.

Sometimes even more challenging than Talking Tammy is Silent Suzy. We must walk a fine line as leaders, not putting on the spot those women who are uncomfortable talking in front of others. I have scared women away by being too direct. So how do we get Silent Suzy to talk without singling her out? Here are some ideas:

- If she is new to the study, don't push her at all during the first few sessions. Let her feel safe and get comfortable. Never call on her to pray out loud or single her out with a pointed question. I once said, "I want to know what Suzy thinks about this." All eyes turned on her, and I'll never forget the tears welling in the corners of her eyes as she said she wasn't comfortable being called on. She didn't come back to the group after that incident. How I wish I could have taken those words back. I learned a valuable lesson from that Silent Suzy—don't push!
- Listen with recall as she answers the All Play question that everyone is asked to answer. Watch for an opportunity to talk about something she has shared with a follow-up question that doesn't pry.
- Take her out for coffee and get to know her. With time, she might warm up and begin to contribute to the discussion. Through a deepened relationship, you'll get a better read on whether you should encourage her to talk.

Challenge #3: Prayer Requests

How often do we run out of time when sharing prayer requests, leaving us no time to actually pray? How do you handle those women who aren't comfortable praying out loud? What if your group has fifteen to thirty women, and just listening to everyone's prayer request takes half an hour?

It's so important to take the time to hear what is going on in one another's lives and to pray for one another. Here are some creative ideas I have learned from others to help keep prayer time fresh:

- As women enter the room, direct them to take an index card or sticky note and write their prayer request on it. Then during prayer time, each woman can read her request aloud, already having thought through it, and pass it to the woman on the right for her to keep in her Bible as a reminder to pray for the request until they meet again.
- Ask someone to record all the prayer requests and e-mail them to the group each week.
- If you have a small group, use a one- or two-minute sand timer when you are short on time. (Look in your game closet for one of these.) Lightheartedly tell each woman that she has one or two minutes to share her request so that each woman can have a turn. (You might want to flip it over again if tears accompany the request.)
- If you have more than ten women, divide into two or three groups for prayer time. Assign a leader who will facilitate, keep the group on track, and follow up. Sometimes our prayer group has gone out for breakfast together or gathered in someone's home to watch the teaching video again.
- Have women pick one or two partners and split into small groups of two or three to share prayer requests and pray for one another.
- Have an open time of popcorn prayer. This means let women spontaneously pray one-sentence prayers as they feel led.
- After everyone shares requests, ask each woman to pray for the woman on her right. Clearly say that if anyone is uncomfortable praying out loud, she can pray silently and then squeeze the hand of the woman next to her.
- Another option is to close the group in prayer yourself or ask a few women you know are comfortable praying in front of others to pray for the requests mentioned. Remember that many women feel awkward praying in front of others. Provide encouragement by reminding the group that prayer is talking to God and that there is no right or wrong way to have a conversation with our Creator. But always be sensitive to others and affirm that they will not be looked down on if they don't like to pray out loud.

Making a change in your prayer time occasionally keeps it from becoming routine or boring. Talking with Jesus should be fresh and real. Taking an intentional, thoughtful approach to this important time of your study will add great value to your time together.

Challenge #4: Developing Leaders

Women's Bible study groups are a great avenue for fulfilling the 2–2–2 principle, which comes from 2 Timothy 2:2: "You have heard me teach things that have been confirmed by many reliable witnesses. Now teach these truths to other trustworthy people who will be able to pass them on to others." God calls us, as leaders, to help raise up other leaders.

Is there a woman in your group who is capable of leading? How can you come alongside her and help equip her to be an even better leader? Wonderful women have invested in me through the 2–2–2 principle, even before I knew that term. As an apprentice, I watched them lead. They gave me opportunities to try leading without handing the reins fully over to me. Then they coached and corrected me. I have since had the privilege of mentoring several apprentices in my Bible study group and watching them go on to lead their own groups. This is multiplying leaders and groups, and God loves it!

Here is the 2–2–2 principle as laid out by Dave Ferguson and Jon Ferguson in their book *Exponential*.[2] (My notes are added within brackets.)

- I DO. You WATCH. We TALK.
- I DO. You HELP. We TALK. [Have your apprentice lead a prayer group or an activity or portion of the session.]
- You DO. I HELP. We TALK. [Ask your apprentice to lead one session with you assisting with facilitation alongside her.]
- You DO. I WATCH. We TALK. [Give your apprentice full ownership for leading a session and resist the urge to jump in and take over.]
- You DO. Someone else WATCHES. [As God leads over time, encourage your apprentice to start her own Bible study group.]

My mentor and I led a Bible study group together for years. As the group grew larger, we both sensed God leading us to multiply the group, forming two groups. It was painful as we missed studying and working with each other. However, God blessed and used both groups to reach more women. Then a woman in my group felt called to lead her own study. She worried that no one would come to her group. She asked many questions as we worked through the 2–2–2 principle. Her first group meeting included eighteen women who now, five years later, still love meeting together. I've seen pictures of them on Facebook enjoying special times together, and I praise God for all that He is doing.

From our one study there are now over five groups of women that meet regularly to study God's Word. This kind of growth begins with commitment to share leadership, follow the 2–2–2 principle, and multiply so that more women can grow in their walk with Christ. Don't miss the opportunity to develop new leaders with intentionality as you model and encourage other women to use their gifts.

Challenge #5: Reaching Out

How do you welcome new women into the group? This is especially tough if yours is an ongoing group that has had the same women in it for years. Newcomers can feel like outsiders if it seems like everyone already knows the unspoken rules of the group. Also, what about those who are finding their way back to God? Are they welcome in the group? While the purpose of the group is primarily Bible study, I've seen the Great Commission of making disciples happen many times through women's groups that meet for Bible study. God's Word will do the transforming work in their lives through the Holy Spirit. We are called to reach out by investing and inviting. Here are some ways a leader can help create an open group:

- End each Bible study with a closing celebration brunch, encouraging the women to bring food and friends. Some ideas for this time together include:
    1. Have an open time when women can share how God worked in their lives through the Bible study.
    2. Have one woman in the group share her testimony of how she came to understand the gospel and how it has been transforming her life recently.
    3. Bring in a speaker from outside the group to share a testimony.
    4. Make it fun! We play a fun group game (such as Fishbowl, Pictionary, or Loaded Questions) and have a white elephant jewelry exchange at Christmas. Women who might think Bible study is a foreign concept can see that you are just a bunch of regular women in pursuit of a supernatural God.
- Leave an empty chair in the group and pray for God to show you someone who needs a group of women she can study the Bible alongside.
- Though the main purpose of the group is Bible study, consider doing a service project together that you can invite other women to participate in (schedules permitting). Our group has made personal care bags for the homeless and also adopted a family at Christmas, which included going shopping for the gifts and wrapping them together. Depending on where God is leading your group, serving together can help put hands and feet to the truths you are learning.
- Socials outside of Bible study also provide an opportunity to invite friends as a nonthreatening transition. While the focus of your group is much more than social, planning an occasional social event can be a good way to forge deeper connections. Our Bible study group has gone bowling together, had a backyard barbecue, and planned a girls' night out at a local restaurant. These times together not only help women get to know one another better but also give them a great chance to invite friends. These same friends who attend a social might later try a Bible study session once they have made connections with some of the women in the group.

Basic Leader Helps

Preparing for the Sessions

- Check out your meeting space before each group session. Make sure the room is ready. Do you have enough chairs? Do you have the equipment and supplies you need? (See the list of materials needed in each session outline.)
- Pray for your group and each group member by name. Ask God to work in the life of every woman in your group.
- Read and complete the week's readings in the participant book, review the session outline in the leader guide. Put a check mark beside the discussion questions you want to cover and make any notes in the margins that you want to share in your discussion time.

Leading the Sessions

- Personally greet each woman as she arrives. If desired, take attendance using your group roster. (This will assist you in identifying members who have missed several sessions so that you may contact them and let them know they were missed.)
- At the start of each session, ask the women to turn off or silence their cell phones.
- Always start on time. Honor the efforts of those who are on time.
- Encourage everyone to participate fully, but don't put anyone on the spot. Invite the women to share as they are comfortable. Be prepared to offer a personal example or answer if no one else responds at first.
- Facilitate but don't dominate. Remember that if you talk most of the time, group members may tend to listen passively rather than to engage personally.
- Try not to interrupt, judge, or minimize anyone's comments or input.
- Remember that you are not expected to be the expert or have all the answers. Acknowledge that all of you are on this journey together, with the Holy Spirit as

your leader and guide. If issues or questions arise that you don't feel equipped to answer or handle, talk with the pastor or a staff member at your church.

- Encourage good discussion, but don't be timid about calling time on a particular question and moving ahead. Part of your responsibility is to keep the group on track. If you decide to spend extra time on a given question or activity, consider skipping or spending less time on another question or activity in order to stay on schedule.
- Try to end on time. If you are running over, give members the opportunity to leave if they need to. Then wrap up as quickly as you can.
- Be prepared for some women to want to hang out and talk at the end. If you need everyone to leave by a certain time, communicate this at the beginning of the session. If you are meeting in a church during regularly scheduled activities or have arranged for childcare, be sensitive to the agreed-upon ending time.
- Thank the women for coming, and let them know you're looking forward to seeing them next time.

Introductory Session

Note: The regular session outline has been modified for this optional introductory session, which is 60 minutes long.

Leader Prep

Materials Needed

- *Elijah* DVD and DVD player
- Stick-on nametags and markers (optional)
- Index cards (optional—Prayer Requests)
- Participant books to purchase or distribute

Session Outline

Note: Refer to the format templates on pages 9–10 for suggested time allotments.

Welcome

Offer a word of welcome to the group. If time allows and you choose to provide food, invite the women to enjoy refreshments and fellowship. (Groups meeting for sixty minutes may want to have a time for food and fellowship before the official start time.) Be sure to watch the clock and move to the All Play icebreaker at the appropriate time.

All Play

Ask each group member to share a little about herself—name, interests, how many Bible studies she's been a part of, and so on.

Distribute the participant workbooks, and then have the group turn to the "Introduction to This Study" (pages 5–8). Ask volunteers to read one paragraph each until you've read through the entire introduction. Point out the different options for study (pages 7–8) and encourage each woman to prayerfully decide what level of study she would like to complete. Decide ahead of time whether you will ask all ladies in your study to take part in the thirty-day prayer challenge or allow them to choose to participate on their own. Ask: Based on this introduction, what are you looking forward to about studying the life of Elijah?

Video

Offer a brief prayer and then play the Introductory Session video.
Discuss:

- What do you already know about Elijah's story? What insights and/or questions did this introductory video raise for you?
- Why is the faith walk more like a marathon than a sprint?
- In what ways is the spiritual life comparable to Olympic training? What practices come to mind that help to build our spiritual stamina and endurance?

- How would you describe your current season of life? Is it a dry and weary season, a season of abundant blessings, or somewhere in between? Explain your response.

Prayer Requests

End by inviting group members to share prayer requests and pray for one another. Use index cards, popcorn prayer, or another prayer technique included in "Tips for Tackling Five Common Challenges" (pages 15–20) to lead this time with intentionality and sensitivity.

Week 1

Prayer

1 Kings 17

Leader Prep

Memory Verse

And it is impossible to please God without faith. Anyone who wants to come to him must believe that God exists and that he rewards those who sincerely seek him.

(Hebrews 11:6)

Materials Needed

- *Elijah* DVD and DVD player
- Stick-on nametags and markers (optional)
- Index cards or sticky notes (optional—Scriptures and Prayer Requests)

Session Outline

Note: Refer to the format templates on pages 9–10 for suggested time allotments.

Welcome

Offer a word of welcome to the group. If time allows and you choose to provide food, invite the women to enjoy refreshments and fellowship. (Groups meeting for sixty minutes may want to have a time for food and fellowship before the official start time.) Be sure to watch the clock and move to the All Play icebreaker at the appropriate time.

All Play

Ask each group member to respond briefly to the following prompt. Read aloud or paraphrase:

- Who is the person you spent the most time talking to yesterday? (This should be a physical person.)

Say something like this after everyone has shared:

- This week we learned about prayer. It can be challenging to have a conversation with someone we can't see or hear, but God invites us to talk with Him. Let's open today by doing just that.

Prayer

Before playing the video segment, ask God to prepare the group to receive His Word and hear His voice.

Video

Play the video for Week 1. Invite participants to complete the Video Viewer Guide for Week 1 in the participant book as they watch (page 47). (Answers are provided on page 216 of the participant book and page 61 of this leader guide.)

Group Discussion

Video Discussion Questions

- How is prayer a contact point between the natural and the supernatural—between us and God?
- Have you ever been in a weary waiting season? What was that like, and what value can you see in it now?
- What is the "impossible request" that you wrote on the chalkboard of your mind?
- Can you name a time when you were persistent in prayer and saw an answer from God?

Participant Book Discussion Questions

Note: Page references are provided for those questions that relate to questions or activities in the participant book.

Before you begin, invite volunteers to look up the following Scriptures and be prepared to read them aloud when called upon. You might want to write each of the Scripture references on a separate index card or sticky note that you can hand out.

Scriptures: Deuteronomy 30:20 and Proverbs 4:13

Day 1: *True Grit*

- What are some things that are wearing you out right now? These aren't necessarily bad or wrong things; they are simply situations, relationships, or routines that require your stamina in this season. (page 15)
- While we can seek God in a variety of ways, prayer is a vital way the Lord has given us to connect with Him. We won't find spiritual stamina apart from prayer. How has prayer helped to build spiritual stamina in your life?
- Jeroboam put his faith in human wisdom rather than God's Word. He sought his own interests rather than closely following God's clear instructions, and His legacy of compromise filtered down to every king who ruled after him. Are there any areas of compromise where you sense God calling you back to a more complete obedience? (page 20)

Day 2: *Calling Us Back*

- What did you learn about the kings of Israel in your readings this week?
- Read Deuteronomy 30:20 and Proverbs 4:13 aloud. According to these verses, what is the key to life? (page 24)

- The Lord is always calling us back to relationship with Him. That's why even when His people completely turned their backs on Him with drunkenness, murder, and idolatry, Yahweh still sent a prophet to call them back. He loved them, and He never gave up on them. When have you experienced God calling you through people, circumstances, thoughts, feelings, the Holy Spirit, or His Word?

Day 3: Hiding Out

- Hiding out doesn't always mean we are scared or in trouble. Some seasons require withdrawing in obedience. Elijah's seclusion provided time for solitude to prepare him for ministry in the years to come. Have you ever sensed God calling you to withdraw from something or someone in obedience to Him? If so, what were some things you discovered about God or yourself during that time? (page 30)
- Another key concept we find in Elijah's story is the supernatural provision of God. How did God provide for Elijah? How has the Lord provided for you in a supernatural or unexpected way at some point in your life—whether it was a physical, spiritual, emotional, or relational need? (page 31)
- The good news is that the Lord wants to walk us through each and every challenge, just as He did for Elijah. How has the Lord walked you through a challenge recently?

Day 4: Changing Providers

- Elijah didn't get a three-year plan for his personal provision when he spoke God's message to Ahab about the drought. As he sought God in prayer, his first instruction was to go east and hide by the Kerith Brook. When has God shown you only one next step at a time?
- Has God ever used an unlikely *place* or *event* to provide for you? (page 35)
- In what area(s) do you need God to give you some reassurance or direction in regard to His provision for you? How is the principle of God's abundant provision in our scarcity hitting home with you? (page 38)

Day 5: When Life Doesn't Make Sense

- During some waiting seasons, I have resorted to watching Netflix and scrolling social media when I feel restless. We have so many choices to fill our time. What is your go-to activity when you're forced to wait? What are some practices that can help build spiritual stamina during a season of waiting? (page 40)
- God invites us to cry out to Him, and I believe He cries with us in the tragedies of life. He is both compassionate and powerful. When things in life don't make

sense, we have two choices: we can give in to despair, or we can continue to cry out to God with shameless persistence. Where is God asking you to grow in prayer? Do you need to work through some disappointments in prayer? Is God calling you to more boldly ask of Him and believe Him? What does that mean for you? (page 45)

- What did you discover about Elijah this week? What about his story is sticking with you?

Optional Group Activity (for a session longer than sixty minutes)

Divide into smaller groups or pairs to review the Weekly Wrap-Up (pages 45–46). Ask small groups to share and discuss their wrap-up statements and one or two ways that they will put into practice something they learned from their readings this week.

Prayer Requests

Invite the group members to share prayer requests and pray for one another. Use index cards or sticky notes, popcorn prayer, or another prayer technique included in "Tips for Tackling Five Common Challenges" (pages 15–20) to lead this time with intentionality and sensitivity.

Week 2

Choices

1 Kings 18:1-40

My session: March 18:

Leader Prep

Memory Verse

Wise choices will watch over you. Understanding will keep you safe. Wisdom will save you from evil people, from those whose words are twisted.

(Proverbs 2:11-12)

Materials Needed

- *Elijah* DVD and DVD player
- Stick-on nametags and markers (optional)
- Index cards or sticky notes (optional—Scriptures and Prayer Requests)

Session Outline

Note: Refer to the format templates on pages 9–10 for suggested time allotments.

Welcome   10:00

Offer a word of welcome to the group. If time allows and you choose to provide food, invite the women to enjoy refreshments and fellowship. (Groups meeting for sixty minutes may want to have a time for food and fellowship before the official start time.) Be sure to watch the clock and move to the All Play icebreaker at the appropriate time.

All Play   10:10 - 10:20

Ask each group member to respond briefly to the following prompt. Read aloud or paraphrase:

This week we explored how our choices impact our spiritual stamina. Over time, bad choices can lead to grave consequences. However, knowing who we are before God and believing that our God loves us and has a purpose for us helps us to choose Him every step of the way. I'm going to give you a few fun choices to make here. Raise your hand for the one (in your opinion) that is the best:

- *Chocolate or fruit dessert?*
- *Beach or mountains for vacation?*
- *Convertible or Jeep?*
- *Giant backyard party or small quiet gathering?*
- *Summer or winter?*
- *Morning or evening?*

Prayer

Before playing the video segment, ask God to prepare the group to receive His Word and hear His voice.

Video   10:20 - 10:45

Play the video for Week 2. Invite participants to complete the Video Viewer Guide for Week 2 in the participant book as they watch (page 79). (Answers are provided on page 216 of the participant book and page 61 of this leader guide.)

Group Discussion   10:45 - 10:05
Video Discussion Questions

- When it seems like life is happening *to* you, how can you shift your perspective to expect that God can work *through* you?
- Do you find it easy or difficult to choose Jesus when offered counterfeit truths or answers to prayer? How do you discern the difference between the movement of Jesus in your life and a counterfeit truth?
- What comes to your mind when you think about God? How does what you think about God impact your choices?

Participant Book Discussion Questions

Note: Page references are provided for those questions that relate to questions or activities in the participant book.

Before you begin, invite volunteers to look up the following Scriptures and be prepared to read them aloud when called upon. You might want to write each of the Scripture references on a separate index card or sticky note that you can hand out.

Scriptures: 1 Kings 18:1-8; 18:9-15; 18:16-19

Day 1: Assurance

- Discerning God's voice can be tough, especially in a world with so much noise. Can you think of a time when you needed assurance that you were headed in the right direction? (page 49)
- Read 1 Kings 18:1-8. Obadiah was an Israelite who felt the same need for confirmation in discerning God's leading that we often experience. He heard God's message from Elijah clearly, but he had some fears and concerns. What do Obadiah and Elijah have in common? How are they different? (page 50)
- Read aloud 1 Kings 18:9-15. Obadiah confessed that he was struggling, and Elijah reminded him that they were on the same team serving a powerful God. Who is your person or people who point you back to God's faithfulness when

you need assurance? How can we all do better about pointing one another to God and encouraging one another with boldness?

Day 2: *Sitting on the Fence*

- Read aloud 1 Kings 18:16-19. Elijah said that Israel's trouble was not outer and circumstantial but inner and relational. He dug below the surface to identify the problem in his land, proclaiming that it was not the lack of rain but the people's lack of faithfulness to God. How would you identify any outer, circumstantial trouble in your world right now? Do you have any inner, relational issues right now? (page 57) How does what troubles us reveal what we value most?
- God calls us to make the choice to fall in love with Him. When we set our hearts and minds to love Him, the disciplines of following Him become less tiring. We find our spiritual stamina building as we choose to imitate His faith, hope, love, and forgiveness. Yet rather than try to do it on our own, we invite the Holy Spirit to do it in and through us. We choose rather than waver. Is there an area in your life where you sense you have been wavering, dabbling in both cultural accommodation and intentional Christian community? (page 60)

Day 3: *Choosing to Challenge*

- The lure of pursuing wealth, prestige, beauty, power, and selfish gain instead of Kingdom priorities can be compared to the Siren song. What are some of the Siren calls of temptation for followers of Christ today? (page 61)
- We often lack clarity concerning the sovereign plan God is unfurling in our lives and the lives of others, but God asks us to trust Him, believing that He will prove Himself real at just the right time. Where do you need clarity right now about whether to speak up, act, or wait? (page 65)
- Sometimes God leads us, like Elijah, to confront the counterfeits we see in the lives of others. But more often God calls us to challenge the counterfeits that deceive and entrap us personally. Have you ever had to call out a counterfeit to someone? What was that experience like? What counterfeits have you been clinging to lately? Think of things that may distract you from God rather than draw you toward Him. (page 66)

Day 4: *Believing in Something*

- Some people embrace the notion that the object of our belief is second to the amount of passion and personal benefit we find in our faith. Do you agree that passion is pointless if the object of our belief is not real? Why or why not? (page 68)

- What are some of the counterfeit gods in our culture today that, regardless of someone's passion, are not real or beneficial?
- What do you think the scene was like when Elijah challenged the counterfeit gods of his day? What might the onlookers have been thinking and saying to one another? What do you think was Elijah's state of mind?
- We can so easily wander off track and find ourselves spending our time, talents, and treasures pursuing counterfeits. What are some practical ways you might draw nearer to God so that you have eyes to see any counterfeits that are deceiving your mind and heart? (page 72)

Day 5: Undeniable

- When have you sensed God's undeniable presence or power in your life? Describe a time when you were assured that God is real and at work in the world—whether it came through circumstances, people, Scripture, church, or something else. (page 73)
- We learn through Elijah's story that spiritual stamina without prayer is impossible. We must talk to God and listen to God. This is prayer, and it is a gift that God offers to us. Is there a specific idea or practice regarding prayer that you sense God calling you to implement? (page 75)
- As Redeemer, God delights to restore relationships. His people had been wayward, serving Baal, a counterfeit god. God's desire was to help them find their way back to Him, and Elijah was His mouthpiece. In your own times of wandering, how has God drawn you back to Him? (page 76)

Optional Group Activity (for a session longer than sixty minutes) 11:05-11:25

Divide into smaller groups or pairs to review the Weekly Wrap-Up (page 78). Ask small groups to share and discuss their wrap-up statements and one or two ways that they will put into practice something they learned from their readings this week.

Prayer Requests

Invite the group members to share prayer requests and pray for one another. Use index cards or sticky notes, popcorn prayer, or another prayer technique included in "Tips for Tackling Five Common Challenges" (pages 15–20) to lead this time with intentionality and sensitivity.

Close @ 11:30

Week 3

Soul Care

1 Kings 18:41–19:18

Leader Prep

Memory Verse

So let's not get tired of doing what is good. At just the right time we will reap a harvest of blessing if we don't give up.

(Galatians 6:9)

Materials Needed

- *Elijah* DVD and DVD player
- Stick-on nametags and markers (optional)
- Index cards or sticky notes (optional—Scriptures and Prayer Requests)

Session Outline

Note: Refer to the format templates on pages 9–10 for suggested time allotments.

Welcome

Offer a word of welcome to the group. If time allows and you choose to provide food, invite the women to enjoy refreshments and fellowship. (Groups meeting for sixty minutes may want to have a time for food and fellowship before the official start time.) Be sure to watch the clock and move to the All Play icebreaker at the appropriate time.

All Play

Ask each group member to respond briefly to the following prompt. Read aloud or paraphrase:

This week we studied the need for soul care in order to maintain our spiritual stamina. What is a favorite way you like to relax? Maybe it's a day at the spa or a lingering meal at a favorite restaurant. This week we saw the importance of allowing our souls to exhale stress and inhale God's grace and goodness. What would your dream soul-care day be like?

Prayer

Before playing the video segment, ask God to prepare the group to receive His Word and hear His voice.

Video

Play the video for Week 3. Invite participants to complete the Video Viewer Guide for Week 3 in the participant book as they watch (page 115). (Answers are provided on page 216 of the participant book and page 61 of this leader guide.)

Group Discussion

Video Discussion Questions

- What is the pace of a typical week like for you? In what ways are you feeling tired or overwhelmed?
- When and how do you make time in your week to care for your soul? To listen for God's still small voice?
- What have you discovered about the unique work God has just for you?

Participant Book Discussion Questions

Note: Page references are provided for those questions that relate to questions or activities in the participant book.

Before you begin, invite volunteers to look up the following Scriptures and be prepared to read them aloud when called upon. You might want to write each of the Scripture references on a separate index card or sticky note that you can hand out.

Scriptures: 1 Kings 18:41-46; 19:1-4; 19:4-5; 19:11-12; Luke 16:10a

Day 1: *Expectant Prayer*

- Read aloud 1 Kings 18:41-46. While no body posture for prayer is prescribed in Scripture, we notice that Elijah assumed a humble position and prayed fervently. What is your typical body posture when you pray? Have you ever prayed while bowing, kneeling, or lying prostrate on the ground? If so, what differences have you noticed when praying in that posture as opposed to praying "on the go"? (page 82)
- Prayer isn't like a vending machine where we tell God what we would like and out comes the package immediately. What is your level of expectation that God will answer? (page 86)
- Elijah prayed for something God had already promised. Although God spoke through prophets in Elijah's day, the promises we can pray with certainty today are found in the Bible. What verses or promises from God's Word have you clung to in seasons of desperation or times of joy? (page 87)

Day 2: *I've Had Enough*

- Read aloud 1 Kings 19:1-4. Elijah knew what it felt like to want to quit. He wanted God to just take him to heaven. Elijah had to learn spiritual stamina in order to keep on going when he felt like quitting. Why do you think Elijah wanted to quit? Have you ever wanted to give up on God? What was that experience like?

- You may or may not be in a low season like Elijah was in our study this week, but we all have things in our lives that can make us grow weary. What is something in your life that is wearing you out right now? (page 92)
- Have you ever felt the need to get away and process the difficulties in your life? Where did you go? How did God show up in those moments? How have you sensed God's comfort and presence in the midst of the brokenness in your life? (page 93)

Day 3: Under the Broom Tree

- Whether our schedules are full of challenging or wonderful things, lack of margin can leave us weary. Do you ever find yourself being forgetful when you feel overwhelmed? What other symptoms do you notice in your life when you are depleted emotionally, spiritually, or physically? How do physical hunger and fatigue affect you spiritually? (page 95)
- Soul-care is vital to our spiritual stamina. Read aloud 1 Kings 19:4-5. What things did Elijah do to take care of his soul?
- How have you witnessed God's provision in your life? What are some present needs that you are praying about right now? (page 99)

Day 4: In the Whisper

- I often want to see God work in remarkable ways, but I am not always willing to obey Him in the small, unremarkable instructions. Read aloud Luke 16:10a. What are some "unremarkable" ways you live for Jesus day to day? How have you practiced being "faithful in little things"?
- Read aloud 1 Kings 19:11-12. Whether we call it a whisper, breeze, or still small voice, God spoke to Elijah in the simple rather than the grandiose. How have you experienced God speaking to you in a "gentle whisper"? (page 105)
- Between the notifications on our phones, the conversations with the people in our lives, and the demands of work, family, and ministry, we don't have a lot of margin for quiet. How can you practically build into your daily routine some time for you to listen to God—not to achieve, or study, or work, but simply to listen for the still, small voice of God?

Day 5: The Toilet Bowl

- While we may not feel like the rest of the world is worshiping counterfeits, many of us have felt on the outside of friendship circles, family groups, church groups, or coworker clusters. Other times we've watched the news of suffering going on around us and questioned if what we do for God's kingdom really matters. Toilet bowl thinking can lead to a place of despair unless we continually realign ourselves with God's grace and hope. What causes your thoughts to go spiraling in your mind, maybe even spinning out of control? How can realigning yourself with God's grace and hope snap you out of that spiral?

- Can you think of a time when you wanted to quit but, after reflection and prayer, God's instructions were to "go back the same way you came"? How did God encourage you as you went back to an old situation with a new attitude? (page 109)

- What is one specific thing God has called you to do that gives you purpose? Are there some ways you sense God calling you to lean into your purpose with greater obedience or clarity? (page 110)

Optional Group Activity (for a session longer than sixty minutes)

Divide into smaller groups or pairs to review the Weekly Wrap-Up (pages 113–114). Ask small groups to share and discuss their wrap-up statements and one or two ways that they will put into practice something they learned from their readings this week.

Prayer Requests

Invite the group members to share prayer requests and pray for one another. Use index cards or sticky notes, popcorn prayer, or another prayer technique included in "Tips for Tackling Five Common Challenges" (pages 15–20) to lead this time with intentionality and sensitivity.

Week 4

Surrender

1 Kings 19:19–22:9

Leader Prep

Memory Verse

Accept the way God does things, for who can straighten what he has made crooked?

(Ecclesiastes 7:13)

Materials Needed

- *Elijah* DVD and DVD player
- Stick-on nametags and markers (optional)
- Index cards or sticky notes (optional—Scriptures and Prayer Requests)

Session Outline

Note: Refer to the format templates on pages 9–10 for suggested time allotments.

Welcome

Offer a word of welcome to the group. If time allows and you choose to provide food, invite the women to enjoy refreshments and fellowship. (Groups meeting for sixty minutes may want to have a time for food and fellowship before the official start time.) Be sure to watch the clock and move to the All Play icebreaker at the appropriate time.

All Play

Ask each group member to respond briefly to the following prompt. Read aloud or paraphrase:

Ice Breaker

> This week we studied surrender. So let's start with a lighthearted question about sweet surrender before we move into discussing a heavy lesson. What was the last delicious treat (salty or sweet) that you surrendered to eating and fully enjoying?

Prayer

Before playing the video segment, ask God to prepare the group to receive His Word and hear His voice.

Video

Play the video for Week 4. Invite participants to complete the Video Viewer Guide for Week 4 in the participant book as they watch (page 153). (Answers are provided on page 216 of the participant book and page 61 of this leader guide.)

Group Discussion
Video Discussion Questions

- When has it been difficult for you to reconcile your theology with your reality?
- What does surrendering to God mean to you?
- How has God's character—His goodness and love—helped you learn to trust Him more?
- Where have you seen glimpses of grace even in the most difficult circumstances?

Participant Book Discussion Questions

Note: Page references are provided for those questions that relate to questions or activities in the participant book.

Before you begin, invite volunteers to look up the following Scriptures and be prepared to read them aloud when called upon. You might want to write each of the Scripture references on a separate index card or sticky note that you can hand out.

Scriptures: Deuteronomy 32:4; 1 Kings 21:1-14; 21:27-29; Psalm 37:23; Proverbs 31:8-9; Jeremiah 32:27; Matthew 28:18-20; Luke 12:7; James 4:8

Day 1: *Clarity*

- In order to develop and maintain spiritual stamina, we must learn to respond to God's grace in the moment even when the harsh realities of life do not make sense to us. This is the surrendered life. How can we take practical steps to move toward a more surrendered life?
- We all need people we can look up to as spiritual examples. Do you have a person of faith whom you have looked to for wisdom? What are some practical ways this person has encouraged you spiritually? (page 119)
- Read aloud Matthew 28:18-20. God has given a common mission to all of us who have chosen to follow Jesus. We are to go, make disciples, baptize, and teach others to obey God's commands. Each of us needs clarity in where, how, and on what timetable we are to fulfill this commission personally; and we must wrestle with God and listen to the voice of His Spirit to know how to apply this command in our lives. What are one or two ways God has called or is calling you to make disciples in your current season of life? (page 121) How can you move forward with a yes to God?

Day 2: *Knowing God*

- We must be careful not to know a lot of stuff about God, the church, and the Bible without *engaging* in a close relationship with the living Christ. What are some different information avenues that you have utilized to learn more about God? What are some truths or actions that have helped you move beyond knowing about God to knowing Him personally? (page 129)

- Read aloud Psalm 37:23; Luke 12:7; James 4:8; and Jeremiah 32:27. Have you ever assumed God wouldn't care about the details of your life because He's too busy with bigger, more global issues? What are some of the big things you are facing and the little things you are concerned about that may seem insignificant in the grand scheme of things? What does it mean to you to know that God delights in the details of your life? (page 131)

- If we want to have spiritual stamina, we must be clear about God's grace, power, and judgment. And as we develop a deep, consistent relationship with Christ, we will be able to love and obey Him in every season of life—even if imperfectly. What are some ways that believers can develop a more consistent relationship with Christ?

Day 3: It's Not Fair

- Read aloud Deuteronomy 32:4. God is just and fair. Because we were created in His image, we have a strong sense of justice. What are some unfair things you have noticed lately? (page 133)

- Read aloud or summarize 1 Kings 21:1-14. What can we learn about God's justice from this story?

- Read aloud Proverbs 31:8-9. Although we cannot fight every battle, we are called to speak up for those who can't speak for themselves and work for justice for those who are oppressed. What are some tangible ways you have seen others get personally involved in speaking up or ensuring justice for others? Are there ways that you also have joined the fight—in the past or more recently? (pages 135–136)

Day 4: The Power of Humility

- Whether it is in your work, ministry, or family relationships, can you relate to the battle with pride when you've done something wrong? (page 138)

- Read aloud 1 Kings 21:27-29. These verses stand out in contrast to the firm hand God had displayed against King Ahab in the past. Here we see the incredible compassion of our God—even toward those we might consider the worst of sinners. As you reflect on Ahab's life and God's willingness to amend Ahab's punishment based on his humility, do any questions arise in your heart and mind? Have you ever seen lack of consequences lead to entitlement or pride in the lives of others? (page 140)

- One principle we find in God's response to Ahab here in 1 Kings 21 is that humility brings out the gracious nature of our God. It often is the same with us. When has your humility increased your awareness of God's grace?

Day 5: *Careful Surrender*

- Ahab hated the prophet Micaiah because he delivered blunt words that usually were not "sunshine and roses." We might be quick to judge Ahab, but the truth is that we tend to like it when people tell us that circumstances will be easy or that we shouldn't feel convicted. Have you noticed a shift among Christians today toward more of a feel-good message? If so, in what ways? (page 147)
- Rather than impulsively accept the loudest voices, the popular voices, or the most convenient voices, we must study, seek, pray, and wrestle to discern God's voice in each situation we encounter. Where is God calling you to listen to His voice even when others around you are accepting counterfeits? (page 149)
- Some things we should always surrender to, such as God's way, God's instructions, and God's grace. Other things we should never yield to, such as counterfeits—things that lead us away from wholehearted living for God. What counterfeits of mainstream culture must we guard against in order to listen to God's voice? (page 149)

Optional Group Activity (for a session longer than sixty minutes)

Divide into smaller groups or pairs to review the Weekly Wrap-Up (pages 151–152). Ask small groups to share and discuss their wrap-up statements and one or two ways that they will put into practice something they learned from their readings this week.

Prayer Requests

Invite the group members to share prayer requests and pray for one another. Use index cards or sticky notes, popcorn prayer, or another prayer technique included in "Tips for Tackling Five Common Challenges" (pages 15–20) to lead this time with intentionality and sensitivity.

Week 5

Mentoring

2 Kings 1–2

Leader Prep

Memory Verse

Never let loyalty and kindness leave you!
Tie them around your neck as a reminder.
Write them deep within your heart.
(Proverbs 3:3)

Materials Needed

- *Elijah* DVD and DVD player
- Stick-on nametags and markers (optional)
- Index cards or sticky notes (optional—Scriptures and Prayer Requests)

Session Outline

Note: Refer to the format templates on pages 9–10 for suggested time allotments.

Welcome

Offer a word of welcome to the group. If time allows and you choose to provide food, invite the women to enjoy refreshments and fellowship. (Groups meeting for sixty minutes may want to have a time for food and fellowship before the official start time.) Be sure to watch the clock and move to the All Play icebreaker at the appropriate time.

All Play

Ask each group member to respond briefly to the following prompt. Read aloud or paraphrase:

This week we took a closer look at Elijah's relationship with Elisha. Who was someone in your teenage years that you looked up to besides your parents? Was there a teacher, coach, extended family member, or friend whom you now recognize was a role model for you during those years whether you realized it then or not?

Prayer

Before playing the video segment, ask God to prepare the group to receive His Word and hear His voice.

Video

Play the video for Week 5. Invite participants to complete the Video Viewer Guide for Week 5 in the participant book as they watch (page 184). (Answers are provided on page 216 of the participant book and page 61 of this leader guide.)

Group Discussion
Video Discussion Questions

- What have your mentors and spiritual friends meant to your walk with God?
- What stands out to you about the relationship between Elijah and Elisha?
- What is the difference between influencing and impacting the lives of others? How have you done both?
- Have you ever considered yourself a mentor to someone? Can you think of anyone in your life right now who might need you to pray for her or spend time with her—whether over coffee or in shared ministry or service?

Participant Book Discussion Questions

Note: Page references are provided for those questions that relate to questions or activities in the participant book.

Before you begin, invite volunteers to look up the following Scriptures and be prepared to read them aloud when called upon. You might want to write each of the Scripture references on a separate index card or sticky note that you can hand out.

Scriptures: 2 Kings 1:9-15; 2 Kings 1:16-17; Ruth 1:6-18; 2 Kings 2:7-14; Hebrews 12:1-2

Day 1: *Is There No God?*

- What has been the most recent troubling circumstance in your life? It could be something small such as an appliance breaking or something big such as a medical diagnosis or job loss. Where did you look for comfort and/or wisdom as you dealt with this circumstance? (pages 157-158)
- What are some things people turn to instead of God for help when something bad happens in their lives? (page 158) What would it mean for Jesus to be Lord of *everything* in your life, and what does this have to do with surrender?
- What are some practices that have helped you build spiritual stamina in your life? (page 160)

Day 2: *Bolder with Time*

- Read aloud 2 Kings 1:16-17. Elijah's bold response essentially delivered his life's message once again, which was to prove the truth of the meaning of his name: *Yahweh is my God.* Our message today is still that Yahweh is God—that He is all-sufficient—both holy and merciful, powerful and compassionate. How have you seen our all-sufficient God working in your life lately (through circumstances, His Word, power over sin, people, etc.)? (page 163)

- Read 2 Kings 1:9-15. As you consider all we have learned about Elijah so far in our study, what do you think might have contributed to the boldness we see in him in these verses? What are some practical steps you might take to live more boldly for God? (page 165)

Day 3: I Will Never Leave You

- Elisha's commitment to Elijah reminds me of the biblical story of Ruth and Naomi. Read aloud Ruth 1:6-18. Both Elisha and Ruth did not listen to their mentor but stayed close through a challenging season. Can you recall a time when you told people you didn't need a meal, some help, or their presence but they showed up anyway? How did you feel about that experience? (page 169)
- Just because something is true does not mean we are obligated to say it. What are some things others have said to you when you were hurting that may have been true but were not helpful? (page 171)
- How has community been an encouragement to you or lifted you up in heavy moments? How have you been part of a community bearing one another's burdens?

Day 4: Chariots of Fire

- What changes would you like to see in your personal prayer life? What is one small step you can implement today to begin working toward that goal? (page 177)
- Read aloud 2 Kings 2:7-14. How do you want to go out? In a blaze of glory or quietly without excitement? How is Elijah's life teaching you about walking through life with God?
- No matter what season you are experiencing right now, you can gain spiritual stamina as you strip off the weight of sin and pursue God one step at a time. Where are you in your walk with God right now? What spiritual disciplines are growing your heart for God? What is God breaking your heart for as you pursue Him?

Day 5: The Power of Pressure

- Nothing can rob of us of spiritual stamina like shame. How does shame rob us of our spiritual stamina? How have you known shame to be a bully in your life?
- The prophets pressured Elisha until he felt ashamed. In what ways have you encountered or witnessed the pressure of others during the past year? (page 180)

- Read aloud Hebrews 12:1-2. Jesus *disregarded* shame; and through His blood shed on the cross and our repentance, we can disregard it too. We are to strip off the sin that weighs us down so that we can run with endurance, keeping our eyes on Jesus. What are some practical ways you can keep your eyes on Jesus in your daily life? (page 182) What are some ways we can be shame-lifters for one another?

Optional Group Activity (for a session longer than sixty minutes)

Divide into smaller groups or pairs to review the Weekly Wrap-Up (page 183). Ask small groups to share and discuss their wrap-up statements and one or two ways that they will put into practice something they learned from their readings this week.

Prayer Requests

Invite the group members to share prayer requests and pray for one another. Use index cards or sticky notes, popcorn prayer, or another prayer technique included in "Tips for Tackling Five Common Challenges" (pages 15–20) to lead this time with intentionality and sensitivity.

Week 6

Legacy

Elijah in the Old and New Testaments

Leader Prep

Memory Verse

We will not hide these truths from our children;
*   we will tell the next generation*
about the glorious deeds of the Lord,
*   about his power and his mighty wonders.*
(Psalm 78:4)

Materials Needed

- *Elijah* DVD and DVD player
- Stick-on nametags and markers (optional)
- Blank cardstock bookmarks and gel pens (optional—Group Activity)
- Index cards or sticky notes (optional—Scriptures and Prayer Requests)

Session Outline

Note: Refer to the format templates on pages 9–10 for suggested time allotments.

Welcome

Offer a word of welcome to the group. If time allows and you choose to provide food, invite the women to enjoy refreshments and fellowship. (Groups meeting for sixty minutes may want to have a time for food and fellowship before the official start time.) Be sure to watch the clock and move to the All Play icebreaker at the appropriate time.

All Play

Ask each group member to respond briefly to the following prompt. Read aloud or paraphrase:

What is something that has been passed down to you from a family member? It doesn't have to be a physical object such as a piece of clothing, furniture, or jewelry—but it could be. Or you might think of a favorite family recipe, skill, or inherited trait.

(Allow responses.)

This week we talked about spiritual legacies. Let's pray together as we prepare to watch our final video teaching from Elijah.

Prayer

Before playing the video segment, ask God to prepare the group to receive His Word and hear His voice.

Video

Play the video for Week 6. Invite participants to complete the Video Viewer Guide for Week 6 in the participant book as they watch (page 215). (Answers are provided on page 216 of the participant book and page 61 of this leader guide.)

Group Discussion

Video Discussion Questions

- How does seeking God's Father-heart help us find healing and purpose in our relationships?
- What does it mean for Christ to increase in our lives as we decrease?
- How can taking the long view help us to leave the legacy we desire?
- What do you think about the image of the spiritual life being a marathon and not a sprint? How does fixing our eyes on Jesus help us pace ourselves and find endurance?

Participant Book Discussion Questions

Note: Page references are provided for those questions that relate to questions or activities in the participant book.

Before you begin, invite volunteers to look up the following Scriptures and be prepared to read them aloud when called upon. You might want to write each of the Scripture references on a separate index card or sticky note that you can hand out.

Scriptures: Malachi 4:5-6 and 2 Peter 1:16-21

Day 1: *Sowing and Reaping*

- As you think about your own family heritage, what are some of the good qualities of your parents and grandparents? (page 189)
- What are some excuses we make for our lack of spiritual fitness? What are you planting with your time and resources; what changes do you feel nudged to make that might benefit your spiritual stamina? (page 191)
- We build a legacy of faith through the good seeds we choose to plant, knowing that some of them will be harvested by future generations. What do you hope those who come after you will remember about you? Describe the legacy of faith you want to leave behind.

Day 2: *The Father-Heart of God*

- Read aloud Malachi 4:5-6. Malachi's prophecy echoed the message Elijah had preached throughout his lifetime: respond to the God who loves you or experience the consequences of separation from God. What did you learn this week about the connection between Elijah, John the Baptist, and Christ?

- How would you explain what it means to "turn the hearts of fathers to their children, and the hearts of children to their fathers"? How does a close relationship with God through Christ affect your family relationships? (page 193)
- All our earthly fathers have imperfections, but God the Father has a love for us that will never fail. What are some words that describe the character of God, our heavenly Father?

Day 3: Mistaken Identity

- When Jesus came on the scene, the Israelite people were desperate for help from Yahweh. Roman oppression and taxes had left them impoverished and controlled. Many devout followers still would have been hanging onto God's promise of rescue through Elijah. Now that you have studied Elijah's life and ministry, why would you guess some people might have thought that Jesus was Elijah? (page 198)
- What stood out to you in the chart of parallels between Elijah and Jesus? Is this a new revelation for you? What is the clear distinction between them that makes it clear that Jesus is not the second coming of Elijah? (Elijah was a man of God; Jesus *is* God.)
- One of the greatest legacies of Elijah is that he points us to Christ. The only way to heal our broken relationship with God and turn the hearts of fathers and children back toward each other is through Christ. His gospel message brings us the stamina we need to continue following God even when we want to quit. Each of us must answer the question Jesus posed to His disciples: "Who do you say that I am?" If someone asked you to describe who Jesus is to you, what would you say? (page 200)

Day 4: Taking the Long View

- How does taking the long view—eternal life kind of long—change the way we handle our time, our money, our relationships, and our spiritual lives?
- Read aloud 2 Peter 1:16-21. Here Peter tells us that we can have great confidence in the message of prophets. We are to pay close attention to what they wrote, because their words come from God and are like a light in the darkness. How has Elijah's story been like a light in the darkness?
- As we think about heaven and take the long view of our circumstances, we too can endure the challenging seasons of life with hope for better days ahead! When you think about heaven, what images come to mind? What are you most

excited about when you think about eternal life in heaven? Can you name some people or activities that help you take the long view when it comes to your spiritual life? (page 205)

Day 5: *Mercy*

- When you have been discouraged either by the response of others or by challenging circumstances, how has the Lord reminded you of His presence and plan? (page 208)
- Though many rejected God in the days of Elijah as well as when God sent His own Son to earth, through God's grace there always has been a remnant, a small group of people who persist in following God. Have you ever thought that the whole world was going its own way and no one seemed to be truly following God? Do you find it easy or difficult to trust God when it seems like you are the only one persisting in following God?
- What points or questions did you star on the summary chart? (pages 210-213) What might change in your life as you commit to build spiritual stamina and apply all you've learned about Elijah?

Optional Group Activity *(for a session longer than sixty minutes)*

To close your study, hand out blank cardstock bookmarks and set out some gel pens or colored pencils. Ask participants to reflect on the memory verses and main points they've studied over the last six weeks. Invite them to write a favorite memory verse, word, or quote from a daily reading. If you have time, ask some volunteers to share what they drew and why.

Prayer Requests

Invite the group members to share prayer requests and pray for one another. Use index cards or sticky notes, popcorn prayer, or another prayer technique included in "Tips for Tackling Five Common Challenges" (pages 15–20) to lead this time with intentionality and sensitivity.

Bonus

Thirty Days of Prayer Challenge

Also see AbingdonWomen.com/Elijah.

I'm so glad you've decided to join me for thirty days of prayer. If you and/or your group choose to participate in this challenge, you will commit to spend ten extra minutes in prayer each day using one of two resources: (1) free downloadable introductions to different prayer methods or approaches, which you may use throughout the thirty days (also printed in full below), or (2) the book 30 *Days of Prayer for Spiritual Stamina* (to download the free resources or order the book, see www.AbingdonWomen.com/Elijah). The idea is to focus on prayer for thirty days using a variety of methods. My hope is that this commitment will provide a place to start and a track to run on for those of us who long to grow in prayer.

Introductions to Prayer Methods

I'm providing a framework for five days of prayer that you will repeat for six sets until you have prayed daily for thirty days. So over a five-day span, you will engage in praying silently, praying aloud, praying through writing, praying with movement, and praying together. Then you will start the process again, going through the five exercises in order so that you are changing your prayer method each day.

1. Praying Silently (Days 1, 6, 11, 16, 21, 26)

Take a few moments to prepare. Turn off all electronics and try your best to minimize anything that might interrupt you for the next few minutes. For silent prayer, I must put my phone and laptop in another room because inevitably I will think of someone I need to text or something I need to look up online as soon as I slow down. Once all distractions are put away, spend about five to ten minutes talking to the Lord.

- Praise Him.
- Confess your sins.
- Thank Him for all He has done.
- Bring your requests before Him.

Then spend at least five minutes in complete silence. For me this takes discipline to slow down and be completely still. If you have a commitment or looming to-do list, you may find it helpful to set a timer. When worries, plans, or thoughts about the day invade your mind, redirect yourself to thinking about God and listening quietly.

2. Praying Aloud (Days 2, 7, 12, 17, 22, 27)

I find it helpful to speak prayers aloud because I am less likely to stop talking mid-thought. I'll admit that sometimes in the midst of silent prayers, my mind can wander off.

Talking out loud helps us make a connection with God that is relational. It's the way we talk to family and friends, and it can be a great way to vary our method of praying to God.

Choose a passage of Scripture to read aloud as part of your prayer time today. Then continue speaking aloud as you praise, confess, and thank God as well as ask Him for everything you need.

Now sit quietly and listen for the Holy Spirit to affirm, guide, and inspire you according to His Word.

3. Praying Through Writing (Days 3, 8, 13, 18, 23, 28)

If you are not a fan of writing things down, I want to invite you to stretch yourself. Some of my friends have shared that they don't want to write their prayers because they would be mortified if anyone ever read them. I understand these concerns. You can hide your journal so it cannot be found, or you can tear out your written prayers and shred or burn them when you are finished. Another idea is to type them on your computer and then immediately delete them. One of the benefits of writing prayers is that it slows us down, giving us time to meditate and reflect—because our minds move faster than our fingers. So grab a journal, notebook, piece of paper, or laptop, and get ready to talk to God, believing that the earnest prayer of a righteous person is powerful and brings great results!

Begin with praise. Take a moment to write a paragraph (at least four sentences) praising God for who He is. Feel free to focus on God's names or character qualities.

Now write a prayer confessing the areas where you are struggling. Sometimes when I am writing out sensitive information, I use first letters of words rather than complete sentences.

Next take some time to reflect and slowly write down what you are thankful for in your life. You can make a bulleted list if you prefer. While you may have many material blessings such as a house, car, and job, consider also people, circumstances, and even difficulties that are developing your character. Identify at least ten things you are grateful for today.

Write out a list of your requests and the needs of others around you.

Don't put your pen down yet. Turn to a blank page in your journal. Sit quietly and focus on God. As you listen, record any encouragements, nudges, convictions, ideas, or Scriptures that come to mind.

4. Praying with Movement (Days 4, 9, 14, 19, 24, 29)

When our children were small, my husband and I taught them to fold their hands in prayer. This wasn't some sort of formula but a way to help them focus and recognize the significance of talking to God. With folded hands, they couldn't bother their siblings or fidget quite as much.

We can talk to God in any position. Many times I silently cry out to God in the midst of other activities—such as during a conversation, while trying to complete a challenging task, or even when speaking on a stage. But as we see in Scripture, people often intentionally change their physical posture for a time of prayer.

In ancient times when people would come before a king, they would kneel to show their humility. Likewise, throughout the Bible we see people kneeling in prayer to show humility before God. Kneeling in prayer was something Jesus did as well (Luke 22:41). In other places in Scripture we find people shouting, dancing, clapping, lifting their hands, bowing down, or lying prostrate as they speak to God. Even today changing our physical posture can help us focus and give an outward expression to our inward attitudes of worship and humility before our Creator.

If you have physical limitations, modify your postures as you pray. Sometimes I skip over instructions such as these for the sake of time or comfort, but I invite you to fully engage in lifting hands, kneeling, and even lying in a prostrate position as you talk to God either silently or aloud.

Some other ideas for your varied postures of prayer include praying while coloring, while doing a simple craft, or while holding a special necklace or object that helps you focus in prayer.

Now choose your posture for listening today. You can take any position that helps you focus on the Lord as you spend some time meditating on what God is speaking to you today.

5. Praying Together (Days 5, 10, 15, 20, 25, 30)

Prayer can be a very personal and private activity. Yet as we find in Scripture, prayer is a spiritual rhythm that is not only private but also shared among believers. Jesus taught that asking in agreement with other believers is powerful: "I also tell you this: If two of you agree here on earth concerning anything you ask, my Father in heaven will do it for you. For where two or three gather together as my followers, I am there among them" (Matthew 18:19-20). We also know that members of the early church were devoted to teaching, fellowship, and prayer (Acts 2:42).

Praying with another person can bring encouragement to both parties. Although we might be hesitant to ask others to pray with us because prayer can be personal and private, we can press through the initial awkwardness and find power and encouragement by praying together.

Take a few minutes to consider someone you can pray with today. Perhaps it is a friend, neighbor, coworker, child, or spouse. Whenever you are able to get together or talk by phone, ask the person for two or three things you can pray for them personally.

Then share a few specific things that he or she can pray for you. As you begin to pray, be sure to praise and thank God before jumping in with the things you are requesting.

If you don't know of anyone with whom you can initiate a brief time of prayer, spend your time asking God to bring you a prayer partner. Ask for boldness to pray alongside others if you struggle with shyness. God has said that where two or three are gathered together as His followers, His presence is sure to be found.

Take some time now to reflect. How did hearing another person pray for your needs encourage you? Was there a sentence or phrase the other person spoke in prayer that caused you to see some of your needs in a different light? As you process your thoughts, feelings, circumstances, and relationships, set your mind on God's Word and character and listen closely.

Video Viewer Guide Answers

Introductory Session
(Optional)

Patriarchs

United

Divided

Israel / Judah

Prophets

Ahab

Jezebel

God

saves

human

Week 1

contact point

waiting

provides

persist

Week 2

through

counterfeits

think

Praying

Week 3

broken / overwhelmed

food / rest

still small / listen

unique work

Week 4

intimacy

mercy

theology / reality

grace

Week 5

counterfeits

caught / taught

showing up

influence / impact

Week 6

healing / purpose

increase / decrease

long view

Notes

1. Paul R. House, *1, 2 Kings, The New American Commentary* (Nashville: Broadman and Holman Publishers, 1995), 209.
2. Dave and Jon Ferguson, *Exponential: How You and Your Friends Can Start a Missional Church Movement* (Grand Rapids, MI: Zondervan, 2010), 58, 63.

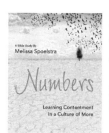

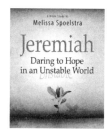

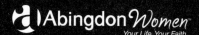

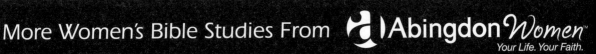
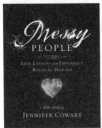

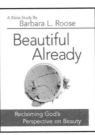

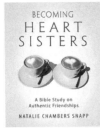